Illus... Pitzer

Additional Copies may be purchased from:
Centering Corporation
P.O. Box 4600
Omaha, NE 68104

Phone: 402-553-1200
Fax: 402-553-0507
www.centering.org

Library of Congress Cataloging-in-Publication Data

Grollman, Earl A.
Talking about divorce and separation: a dialogue between parent and child / by Earl
Grollman ; illustrated by Susanna Pitzer.
p. cm.
"A Centering Corporation resources".
Updated ed. of: Talking about divorce. 1975.
ISBN: 1-56123-155-X (alk. paper)
1. Divorce--United States--Juvenile literature. 2. Parent and child. 3. Children of
divorced parents--Juvenile literature. 4. Divorced parents--United States--Juvenile
literature. [1. Divorce.] I. Pitzer, Susanna. II. Grollman, Earl A. Talking about divorce.
III. Title.

HQ834.G76 2005
306.89--dc22

2005050181

A DIALOGUE BETWEEN PARENT AND CHILD

Talking About Divorce and Separation

A Centering Corporation Resource

By Earl A. Grollman

Originally published by Beacon Press, 1975
Edited by Andrea Gambill

A NOTE TO PARENTS

You are now walking down the lonely road of separation and divorce. How will you tell your child that you will no longer live together as a family?

The pages immediately following this preface are written with the hope that you and your youngster will be sympathetically guided toward honest understanding of the meaning of separation and divorce.

Before you begin the family dialogue, first read the Parents' Guide beginning on page 32. You will obtain the best results when you have carefully decided what material in the children's text should be stressed and how it can be presented to your child.

Success will not depend solely on the spoken word. It is you who must make the child believe that you are still vitally concerned about his or her future. The child should sense that you are not only an understanding reader, but also a caring listener.

Even though you and your spouse will walk separate paths, the challenging task is to demonstrate to your youngsters both by word and by touch that you remain parents and will love them always.

Earl A. Grollman

You know
Mommy and Daddy have not been getting along,
don't you?

How many times have you heard us arguing?

Now, everyone argues from time to time.

Just like you and your friends.

People have differences.

It is natural to be angry sometimes.

It is not always wrong to raise your voice
and lose your temper.

But for us, your parents,
we do not just have a little fight.

We seem to be arguing all the time.

You can tell by the way we are picking on each other.

You see Mommy crying, sometimes.

You know Daddy is not home
like he used to be.

Sometimes one of us leaves right after a quarrel.

Have you noticed this?

The reason is because Mommy and Daddy
are no longer happy with each other.

That's why we are sad.

And not only are we mean to one another,
sometimes we YELL at you for no good reason,
even when it isn't your fault.

It's like when you don't get a good night's sleep.

The next day aren't you grumpy?

You just don't feel right.

That's the way it is with Mommy and Daddy.

We aren't happy with each other.
We don't want to live together.
We have decided to separate.

We know it hurts you to hear this.

You've watched us.
You've seen how we are, haven't you?

This is why we decided not to stay together anymore.

This is called SEPARATION.
It is when Mommy and Daddy will no longer
live in the same house together.

Why are we doing this?

It is not because you have done anything wrong.

You are NOT the reason
for us wanting to live away from each other.

Do you understand?

You bring us HAPPINESS
even when many things in our marriage are wrong.

You are the WONDERFUL
part of our lives.

You are NOT to blame for the separation.

YOU ARE NOT TO BLAME.

Do you think you are? Who is to blame?

Mommy and Daddy are not perfect.
We've both made mistakes.
We are sorry. More than you know.

We know how unhappy you are.

Tell us how you REALLY feel.

We will listen.

We WANT to know.

When something happens,
people do many things.

Some want to SCREAM at the top of their lungs.

And some just want to be alone.

Are you frightened?

Are you angry?

It is all right to let go of some of your feelings.
You may feel better if you do.

But no matter what you do,
Mommy and Daddy will no longer live together.

We thought about it for a long, long time.

Our marriage is not a good one.

It is a mistake.

Sometimes the way to correct a mistake
is to make a change.

And, the way we will change is by living apart.

And probably, after a while
we will get divorced.

Even though we will no longer be husband and wife,
we will still be your Mommy and Daddy.

We are your parents.
We will take care of you the best way we know how.

That is the one thing both of us agree on.

You are our child and we will LOVE YOU always!

A Parents' Guide to Talking About Divorce and Separation

Marriage has been described as the one enterprise which we expect 93 percent of people to enter and 100 percent to be successful.

Not all marriages are successful. Perhaps this is why you are reading this book. You are contemplating divorce. You are justifiably concerned and apprehensive. To you it means an end to your cherished hopes and dreams. To your child it could seem like the end of the world. How are you going to face the turbulence of this frightening experience? Is there a good way to break the news to the youngster?

Most of the volumes written for children of divorce have been narratives about a mythical Dick and Jane - stories about fictional characters, novel descriptions of other children.

Talking About Divorce and Separation: A Dialogue Between Parent and Child is about real people, namely you, the readers. You are about to tell your child how your separation and divorce will touch and change your customary family living. You will tell the youngster just what the divorce will mean in terms of his or her future. Equally important in the dialogue is your encouragement to your child– your willingness to share your child's real feelings, whether it be anger, resentment, hostility or just plain relief that an unhappy family is breaking up. Whatever your child's emotions at this critical time, you all must now try to communicate the best way you know how.

While insight is a gift, you, the parents, must now place yourselves in a position to receive it. You should prepare yourselves for it. Observe your children and hear the tone and timbre of their voices. Let the youngsters tell you how they feel, what they think, what they wish to know.

In order to prepare yourself for this dialogue, first absorb the contents of the children's read along section. Then read and reread this guide. Determine in advance the best method of interpreting the material to your child: what points to emphasize, what lessons to underscore. Anticipate problems not discussed in these pages. Where will your child now live? With whom? What about visitations? Even if the details of your divorce are not complete, let your child know that you are working out the arrangements and will always keep him or her informed of developments.

In your discussion, honesty is the only policy. One of the worst problems for the child is lack of understanding because of parental secrecy. Once the matter is out in the open, it can be faced, for then it is not quite so frightening. You only hurt your child when you deny him or her the opportunity of facing a painful but necessary reality of life. The worst actuality is often preferable to uncertainty.

Difficult as it may be, this book should, if possible, be read with both parents present. This would serve many purposes. It lessens the possibility of one partner's making the other the culprit. In a united explanation you indicate an attempt to work for the best welfare of your child. This means not letting your youngster become a weapon in the battle between the parents or asking the child to take sides. It connotes a shared interest. Obviously, in some circumstances, both parents cannot be present for the family dialogue. One can only do one's best under existing circumstances.

The conversation should not take place after husband and wife have been arguing. Too often in an atmosphere of heated anger, the hysterical parents rush headlong to the youngster with *"We can't stand it any longer! We're getting divorced!"* Separation and its meaning should be approached gently and sympathetically during a time of relative relaxation and tranquillity. Make sure the house is quiet and you have ample time to be alone with the family.

This book is not designed to be read in one sitting. Many children are not able to absorb this information quickly.

Try to answer questions with the most appropriate factual response. Speak *with* the youngster, not at him. All children need to talk, not just be talked to. Converse in such a way as to encourage the ability, both your child's and yours, to think, digest and understand what is significant in what each says.

Try to discern the child's real concerns. The deeper problem may not appear at first. Each of us, whether child or adult, lives in a different perceptual world; we see and construct our pictures of the universe in terms of our own needs and emotional experiences. We must realize that each person has his own, unique way of viewing or framing a view of the world around him.

One of the great rights you can give your child at this time is the right to feel. Never turn away from his or her thoughts or brand them as *"insignificant"* or *"childish."* Allow resentment and guilt to wither in the sunlight rather than attempt to pull them out by the roots by condemning your child for genuine emotions.

The youngster may ask you to repeat the explanation. Even adults who hear of a crisis may say, *"I don't believe it. It can't be true."* So, gently, say it again. The child's need of repeated explanation is his way of coping and working through the perplexing situation.

What is said is important, but how it is said has even greater bearing on whether the child will develop neurotic anxiety or accept, within her capacity, the fact of separation. The best explanation is often nonverbal. If you hold the youngster close to you, he will feel your warmth and really know that she is not being abandoned.

Equally important, you as parents must realize that your divorce does not mean you have forsaken your child. Know that a youngster is better off in a broken home than an unhappy one. A marriage that is doggedly maintained "for the sake of the children" could create more severe problems, not only for you but, through you, for the youngster. A child living with disturbed parents more often gets into psychiatric difficulty than one whose parents have been strong and mature enough to sever their unfortunate relationship.

DISCUSSION QUESTIONS:

Page 4

"You know Mommy and Daddy have not been getting along, don't you?"
Separation is the honest admission that husband and wife are not happy with each other and no longer wish to live together. There is no reason to pretend otherwise. Initially, it seems easier to respond to the agony of breakup with untruths. But if you expect your child to be honest with you, you must be honest with him or her. Ultimately, lying leads to confusion, misconception and distrust. Evasions indicate your own inability to handle this stressful situation.

Page 5-6

"People have differences. . . It is natural to be angry sometimes."
Language has different meaning for parents and children. The youngster hears the words "anger," "rasing your voice," "losing your temper," and in the future could associate these phrases with painful separation. Let him or her know that it is only natural to have arguments. One is not bad because of angry thoughts and feelings. But make the distinction between the playmates' infrequent squabbles and the parents' constant, intense disputes.

Page 8-11

"You see Mommy crying sometimes. You know Daddy is not home like he used to be. Sometimes we yell at you for no good reason."
It is futile to believe that your prolonged upheaval has remained a secret. Even the very young person senses frightening changes taking place. When there is tension, the child experiences parental depression. Very often, he or she perceives the inevitability of divorce even before the parents have reached this conclusion.

Page 20

"You are not to blame for the separation. You are NOT to blame. Do you think you are? Who is to blame?
The child may believe that they must be responsible for the separation. After all, in their limited experience, unfortunate things happen when someone is naughty. So they search for the terrible act that caused the breakup. To them, divorce must be some punishment for wrongdoing. An unreasoning guilt drives the child into self-pity and even self-punishment.

Say again and again that you are unhappy with each other but not with them. The reason for the divorce is not because the child was bad. As long as he or she believes that they have caused the separation, they can conjure up the illusion that they have the power to bring you all back together again.

"Mommy and Daddy are not perfect. We both made mistakes."
A youngster often believes that the separation must be his or her fault. Many children think parents are perfect. Therefore, the fault must lie with the child.

It is important for the child to realize that adults are not all-powerful and all-knowing. You demonstrate the highest maturity when you acknowledge that you make mistakes. It is the reward and penalty of being human not only to err but to admit weakness.

"Tell us how you really feel. We will listen. We want to know. It is all right to let go of some of your feelings. You may feel better if you do."
A child's emotional response is a complicated mechanism. He is distressed that one parent will now leave the household. The familiar design of family life is disrupted. The youngster may even believe that he was magically selected for personal pain and punishment.

How the child reacts depends on many factors: age, custody arrangements, coping mechanisms, previous relationship with parents. Each child experiences the conflict in a different way, for each child's response is unique. If the parents do not tell the truth and the child is not permitted to express his feelings, the following are some symptoms divorce could provoke.

Denial and Silence

The young employ the mechanism of denial to protect the ego from disagreeable circumstances. The reaction to the trauma of divorce might be, *"I don't believe it. My parents are just having another argument. They would never leave me."* The ability to deny unpleasant parts of reality is the counterpart of an hallucinatory wish fulfillment. In a sense, it amounts to closing one's eyes to the real state of affairs.

Older youth, also, may not tell the truth about family situations. Studies reveal that many students often lie about their family after their parents are divorced and talk as if their mother and father were still living together.

Regression

Following the traumatic experience of divorce, the youngster might retreat to earlier stages of development. They could return to infantile tendencies belonging to the period preceding the conflict. Regression is the result of failure to master new anxiety. He or she is just afraid to take the next step and may feel more secure when he retraces his steps back to the time of safety before the breakup. In a primitive return to earlier forms of gratification, speech often becomes babyish. Or he may suck his thumb, wet the bed, and whine a great deal to demand attention. It's like saying, *"I'm just a little baby again. Don't leave me. Stay together."*

Bodily Distress

Psychological anxiety is sometimes accompanied by physiological change: trembling, restlessness, loss of appetite, an increase in pulse and respiration rates, nausea, diarrhea, urinary frequency, and fitful sleep which may be interrupted by frightening dreams. Sometimes these dreams become so threatening that the child believes himself in danger. No longer is she sure that food, shelter and comfort will be forthcoming. His reactions may also be an unconscious method of trying to unite the parents to take care of the now-sick child.

Hostility

The child is threatened with separation and loss of love. He or she wants revenge. When enraged, the first impulse is to strike the person or persons who caused so much pain. (Some parents may not like hostility in themselves but just will not tolerate it in children.)

The youngster may interpret the breakup of the home as a form of abandonment. She feels that he has been betrayed by those he loves best and needs the most. She wishes to retaliate by getting even. She may become so furious that he attempts to destroy everything around him, and eventually himself.

Some parents unwisely react to this anger by threats of further punishment. But the young person has had enough abuse. Let him know that you understand feelings of resentment. Listen to him if he tells you about his. Encourage him to express his feelings and answer his questions frankly and lovingly.

Crying

Crying is a natural expression. The child is anxious and guilty–anxious because his future is being threatened, guilty because of an actual or imagined role in the domestic strife. He may cry as he expresses this painful emotion. When his tears flow, he feels better. He experiences pain but does not know how to verbalize it. Tears make up for words.

The worst possible response is for the youngster to repress his feelings. An individual who stoically keeps his grief bottled up inside may later find release in a more serious psychological explosion.

Be realistic enough to say, *"I know you are crying because you care so much. You feel strongly because you love us and are afraid."* In this way you allow him or her the opportunity of relieving tension. Otherwise the adult deprives the child of giving expression to the true emotion of the sadness of separation.

Page 26-27

"Sometimes the way to correct a mistake is to make a change. And the way we will change is by living apart."
Life's challenges are the personal choices available to all of us. One profits from yesterday's experiences by learning to pursue new meanings for tomorrow.

Page 27

"And probably, after a while we will get divorced."
In a desire to appease the youngster, some adults attempt to soften the blow by saying, *"Maybe we will think it over again."* So the hope against hope that perhaps his parents will not be divorced is allowed to remain. Once again, when the decision is irrevocable, honesty is the only formula. Things cannot be changed; the parents will not be reunited. Help the child to deal with life's realities. The truth is that the separation is unalterable.

"We are still your parents. We will take care of you the best way we know how."
The child of divorce still has two parents. You are both alive and well and care
deeply about your child. After the separation, he or she may even be surprised
to discover that the house is happily quiet for the first time. The youngster can
perhaps spend more creative time with his parents than ever before. Now that the
tumult and the shouting have disappeared, the individual parent and child may be
more able to rediscover one another. Distance does not have to diminish love.

SOME FINAL THOUGHTS

Some parents try to make up for their absence or compensate for their guilt by giving their children everything they want. Every trivial demand becomes a compelling
command. A steady flow of expensive but unnecessary gifts pours in. In addition,
the parents continue to spoil the child by doing only "fun things" and failing to
discipline the child when necessary. They try to buy affection by being the "good
guys." They do not understand that love cannot be purchased.

Don't try to "make-up" by overindulgence. A child needs to bend efforts toward
achievement, but overindulgence deprives the youngster of attaining satisfactions by
his own efforts. Nor should he or she be subject to the parents' recurring personal
hostility. The child should never be treated as an unwanted burden, a perpetual
source of trouble. Let the youngster receive the privilege of growing up, occasion-
ally being naughty and mischievous. Parents should be neither too demanding nor
too permissive. The goal is balance—something never easy for parents under any
circumstances.

Divorced parents should avoid the temptation of making the child a substitute
adult or surrogate partner. A youngster does not replace the absent mate. Physi-
cal intimacy such as sharing a bedroom should be tactfully avoided. Seductive and
sexually stimulating situations cause embarrassment and guilt. Your child is not
your lover-companion-confessor-spouse. He should be accepted within the limits of
his psychological and intellectual capabilities. He is still a child.

Often one mate will blame the other entirely for the trouble in the marriage. When one parent is disparaged, the child is forced into a painful choice, having to take sides. In the bitter contest for the child's affection and the parent's exoneration, such statements are frequently heard: *"Your father never cared for you"* or, *"Your mother is selfish and only thinks about herself."* The child is "used" in this vendetta as a means for transmitting adult contempt and retribution. The result is the youngster's further insecurity. After all, no one likes to think that his father is completely unfeeling; no one wants a self-indulgent mother. The youngster may feel that it is hopeless to even try to be good, that this is his psychological inheritance–doomed to be bad, just like his parents.

The child needs to feel wanted and loved, by two parents who are neither saints nor villains. She experiences an intolerable hurt when her mother and father say anything denigrating about the other. Is there any reason to blacken each other's character and then ask the youngster to judge between weaknesses? Such a feud only keeps alive bitterness and misunderstanding. If you need revenge, you are not completely free from your former mate.

On the other hand, don't go overboard in the opposite direction. You do not have to stress the other's virtues. The child perceives duplicity and loses faith in the parent who tells him what he knows to be false. He thinks, *"If he or she was so wonderful, why are they getting divorced?"*

Nor do you need to go into minute detail about all the reasons for divorce. Remember, you are speaking to a child, not your therapist. It is neither necessary nor wise to isolate single issues. In an effort for honesty, one mother tried to explain the motive for divorce by saying, *"We just can't agree on money. I want to buy clothes and Daddy won't let me."* Now, financial difficulties were one of the causes for the division between this husband and wife, but by trying to be specific, the mother oversimplified the problem. The child responded, "I'll tell you what. Keep my allowance. I won't buy any candy. This way we can all stay together." Events described individually seem trivial and surmountable. The single conflict is only a symptom of the over-all, complex source of disharmony. You might instead say, *"You have watched us for so long and you have seen us unhappy for so many reasons."*

What if the mate runs off and shows no interest in the child? The other parent should acknowledge this reality and help the youngster come to grips with it. Even under these circumstances, however, it is not necessary to portray the other party as a completely wicked individual. Did you not marry him or her for his or her good points? What were they? Let the child respect traits that deserve praise and genuinely acknowledge faults. In short, do not paint a false picture of either the other's perfections or shortcomings. Try to place the love for your child above the resentment for your mate. The truth is that both parents are human.

For both adults and child, being human means living with problems. There are times when even the best-informed and well-intentioned are simply inadequate. Seeking help from a therapist, psychiatrist, psychologist, or a child-guidance clinic is not an admission of weakness, but a demonstration of real love and strength.

Some danger signals that indicate that professional assistance should be considered include: delinquency, unwillingness to remain in school, difficulties in learning, sexual perversion, obsessive-compulsive reactions, tics, as well as withdrawal and unfriendliness.

This is a time of stress and strain and your discussions with a sympathetic but objective professional may help not only your youngster but yourself as well.

It is important for you as parents to recognize your own anxieties. Regardless of what you say, your emotional feelings are transmitted to your child. Your capacity for empathy with the child can be blocked by your own personal distress at the time of separation.

You will get discouraged. At best, it is not easy to raise youngsters. Remember, everyone gets depressed during difficult periods of transition. Just as you don't demand too much from the youngster, so you should not create unrealistic requirements for yourself. Goals must be flexible. Take one day at a time. Accept what little you can do at the moment, even as you strive to accomplish a little more in the future. If you reject yourself as a failure, you will only create a more difficult environment for yourself and your child.

You can only bring alive an outlook that is authentic for you. The actual words you use are less important than the attitude you convey. It is only as you now search and find answers for yourself that you will help your child to search and find answers for himself or herself. This will demand your best wisdom, your most creative efforts. For the real challenge is not just how to explain separation and divorce to your child but how to make peace with it yourself.

About the Author

Dr. Earl A. Grollman is a writer, lecturer, and rabbi whose pioneering in the field of crisis intervention has helped thousands of people.

His work on grief and loss is legendary whether it be on separation and divorce, death and dying, or caring for a loved one with Alzheimer's. His appearances on Fred Rogers' Neighborhood culminated in the highly acclaimed published pamphlet by Fred and Earl entitled, *Talking With Families About Divorce*.

Dr. Grollman is a frequent speaker appearing at schools and universities, clergy institutes, medical forums, hospital nursing associations and hospice and support groups throughout the world.

About the Illustrator

In addition to her work as an artist, Susanna Pitzer is the author of several books for children, including: *Grandfather Hurant Lives Forever*, published by Centering Corporation and *I'm Not Afraid of Dogs*, coming out in 2006 from Walker and Company.

She has also written many plays, including: *Grimm Sisters, Can You Hear the Talking Dog?* and *Traveling Through Dreams*.

Susanna lives in New York City with her three shelties, Zzazu, Sofie, and Daisy.